Camping Diaries

The good life and the
not so good life

Compiled by
Christie Marie

Copyright © 2026 by Christie Marie Krull
All rights reserved.

This book is protected by copyright law and international treaties, including the Berne Convention and Pan-American copyright agreements. No part of this publication may be reproduced, distributed, transmitted, or stored in any form or by any means—electronic, mechanical, photocopying, recording, or otherwise—without prior written permission of the copyright holder, except for brief quotations used in reviews or scholarly works.

ISBN: 978-1-971150-00-0

This work is a memoir-based family anthology. All of her six children, her sister, husband, mother, and a future daughter-in-law responded to Christie's request for a story in place of a Christmas gift. So, in came the emails filled with reflections and stories of camping adventures. Several are hilarious, others are more pensive and reflective of times spent in nature and with family. Certain names, places, and identifying details may have been altered to protect privacy.

christiemariebooks.com
Printed in the United States of America

DEDICATION

To all of my family and to all who dare to dream of a simpler life. To those who have pulled out all of the stops and have actually taken the plunge to go without modern luxuries to get in touch again with nature, their true selves, and those cherished people, without the distractions of this modern world. Come taste a raw sample of the dressed-down times of a few adventurous wanderers.

PREFACE

    This idea for stories based on wilderness camping experiences had been on my bucket list for several years. I wrote down a few, but I grew curious about the travels of my six children and others in my family. Each has a different perspective, and I wanted to hear about their journeys off the grid as well.

    In the summer of 2025, I texted my first summons in our family chat, hoping that others would see the value of putting their unique travels out there in print for others and their posterity to enjoy. Well, I waited patiently at first. I sent another reminder of my idea for this project. Crickets.

    You see, each member of my family is talented at expressing themselves, whether in writing or speech. I have observed them through the years. I know these things. I kept dreaming of the wealth of stories and adventures that would pour into my inbox, but to no avail.

    Corporate, government jobs, building a home, many mouths to provide for, starting up new jobs with challenging learning curves, moving and making adjustments in new vocations while taking university classes, driving hundreds of miles a week pursuing sales, retired and comfortable with life, and my ninety-five year old mother feeling a bit insecure about writing anything under the roof of me, a published blogger with several books in process.

    In October, I was organizing and packing for conferences I would teach during our month-long trip with a total of eighteen *reuniones*, meetings in cities, and in many remote rural areas of Costa Rica. I debated on whether or not to take on the extra weight of my trusty computer for the half days here and there when I wasn't in transit for hours traveling to the day's destination or needed to (poorly) translate for my husband when we had team members or friends who did not speak English in our apartment or sharing a meal.

I kept thinking about several writing projects I had in limbo, waiting for me to finish. Which ones would I concentrate on? Again, I reached out with a wistful reminder to put down in words some memories from camping that others would love to read. Not one taker.

Upon returning from our trip, I was thrown into preparations for several family members who would be houseguests over Thanksgiving week. Gratefully, we scheduled a cleaning crew to lighten my workload so I could unpack, do laundry, plan menus, shop, and then enjoy soaking up all our dinners at various homes, picnicking, and hiking at Lost Maples State Natural Area.

Our family gatherings continued throughout the week. In the back of my mind, I reflected on how beautiful all of our lives are. Tough times for us all for sure, but such vibrant lives chatted, laughed, and sat before me.

As I sat there, I wanted to know them better, on a more intimate level that only one-on-one conversations deliver or long social media posts, memoirs, or, yes, I needed to have a new strategy to draw out and unveil all of these wonderful people to the world.

Then one evening, the answer came to me: I would ask them for a simple, inexpensive Christmas gift, a story. So, I wrote out my simple request. *Please, I only want one thing for Christmas. Write me a camping story.* Easy, right?

Hesitant replies slowly came my way one by one. Excuses, faltering around to let me know they heard, but unbelief seemed to hang back, tapping on their shoulders. There were so many more important and pressing things to do this time of year. *Maybe.*

My busiest daughter sent hers in first. I read it aloud to my husband. I reminded him of a story he used to tell about a campout in the mountains with friends as a teen. He caught the bug and promised me a story.

Late that night, I caught him at his computer, pecking away, and when I looked at him wonderingly, he proudly exclaimed that he was getting my Christmas present ready. I was overjoyed that he cared to follow through. His comfortable mode of communication was in the spoken word. He kept us all laughing with his jokes, stories, and recollections. I was so proud of him.

Then my ninety-five-year-old mother brightened when I encouraged her to write about a trip we never let her forget.

"Really? You think I can do this?" She queried.

"Sure, you can, and I will edit and help you turn your thoughts into a great story," was my instant reply.

As I talked and kept reminding my kids of memories, one by one, the stories appeared in my email, tagged *Here you go!* with an attachment. Again, I shared the stories with my husband and mother. I loved each one. Different styles, outlooks, but each a gem for these eyes to behold.

Don't let some of our misadventures scare you off from trying your hand at camping. For most of us, there is nothing better than unplugging for one or two weeks. We have a few episodes you can learn from, but if you do your research and come equipped, you are sure to make some great memories, build strong connections, and have photos to prove you were really out there.

I hope you enjoy our stories almost as much as we enjoyed the journey through memory lane. Maybe you would like to add your own outdoor adventure for a future volume. Just send it through my website: christiemariebooks.com. I would love to read and relive them all with you.

Go off-grid for a while. Reset and refocus. Get in touch with the real you. It is invaluable time well spent. Happy traveling and enjoy life.

CONTENTS

The Great Shady Lake Detour.................................13

A Beary Scary Night....................................19

Headed South: Kodiak...............................25

The Cliffside Scare: A Secret from Lake Superior...33

A Crumby Night...37

An Arkansas Mini-Adventure......................41

Camping on Horseback..............................45

Once and Never Again................................49

Hill Country Adventures: The Vision........................55

Hill Country Adventures: Exploring.......................59

Hill Country Adventures: The River.......................63

Hill Country Adventures: Gratitude.......................67

Chasing Freedom......................................71

To the Center of the Universe....................75

A Camping Misadventure...........................83

Bear Tracks..89

THE GREAT SHADY LAKE DETOUR
By Audrey Keel

There's a particular kind of courage that shows up when you load four kids into a van, point it toward a national forest, and decide you're going to make memories even though life has recently been rearranged in ways no one dreamed of six months before. I didn't feel especially brave at the time.

Mostly, I felt tired from paperwork, carrying the low hum of responsibility in my body, yet quietly determined to give my kids one last golden summer of long roads and shared laughter before full-time work and public schooling claimed more of our days.

That summer was our first series of solo road trips together, just me and my older four, a small traveling circus of laughter, backseat negotiations, and overconfident playlists, carried forward by a belief that adventure could still find us if we stayed open enough to let it.

On our very first trip, the second night was meant to land us early at Shady Lake in the Ouachita National Recreation Area, with plenty of daylight to explore and settle in gently. Instead, Google Maps decided we needed a stronger initiation.

We followed the blue line through winding forest roads until it proudly announced we had arrived, which turned out to be a large metal gate plastered with signs declaring *Private Property*, *No Exit*, and absolutely nothing that suggested a campground lived beyond it. At the exact same moment, our cell service vanished entirely, leaving us alone with the trees and our collective blinking disbelief.

The kids looked at me from the backseat, "What do we do now? We don't have a map."

I took a breath and said the first thing that felt steady and true, "We're gonna do what we did when I was a kid. We're gonna find someone to ask for directions."

I turned the van around and drove back toward the only house that I remembered seeing, one that sat closer to the road with a wraparound porch and a gated yard that felt at least potentially welcoming. I pulled up, told the kids to stay put, and stepped out, only to be immediately greeted by two large dogs charging at the gate, barking to make their position very clear.

I calmly returned to the van and waited. After a minute or two, unsure how else to announce ourselves, I gave a gentle honk that felt vaguely rude but deeply necessary.

Shortly after, a man stepped out of the house and began walking toward us, friendly and cautious in equal measure: "What can I do fer ya?"

I explained the GPS mishap, the disappearing signal, and our sudden introduction to a gate that very much did not want us to enter. He nodded as if this were a familiar story, then gave us perfect directions the old way, with turns and bends, and a confidence that came from knowing the land through his experience rather than consulting a screen.

Photo by Audrey Keel

Five minutes later, we were rolling into Shady Lake. We filled out the self-check-in envelope, slid our fee into the metal box, and then paused to read the posted warnings, which included detailed instructions about black bears, food storage, and what to do if one wandered by. I stood there absorbing this information with a polite nod, holding bear mace and a small bell I planned to wear so we wouldn't surprise anything large, while privately wondering how Arkansas had suddenly become this adventurous.

As we drove deeper into the campground, another realization arrived quietly: We were the only ones there. No tents. No lanterns. No other cars. Just us, the lake, and the forest easing into the night. I took stock: No cell service + middle of nowhere + single mother + four kids under age eleven = not the best idea ever. Yep, it didn't add up to wisdom.

The light was fading fast, and I could tell we had maybe twenty minutes to pitch the tent and get a fire going before darkness took over completely. Thankfully, I had practiced once before, back in our backyard during a very enthusiastic s'mores-fueled campout involving cousins and neighbor kids, so my hands remembered what to do even if my nerves were humming.

I laid out the tarp and tent and asked the kids to grab the edges and pull, then handed the support rods to the older two while sending the younger two off to gather kindling for the fire. The tent rose just as the last light slipped away, and I turned the van headlights toward our site so I could stake it down enough to survive the night, skipping a few stakes once hunger complaints began to reach critical mass.

Dinner came together quickly. Hot dogs skewered over the fire, chips and fruit passed around, the smell drifting beautifully into the woods... too beautifully. A raccoon charged straight at us, fully convinced he had been invited.

The lesson was immediate. Eat fast and put everything away before anything bigger with fangs shows up. I hurried the kids through their food, bagged the trash, and carried it to the farthest receptacle, taking the bear mace along and practicing a quick spray on a tree, just in case theory needed to become skill put to use later that night.

Back at camp, food went into the cooler and back into the van, voices bubbled upward toward the treetops and stars, and despite the nerves, there was laughter. Because of our late arrival, there would be no exploring that night, so we walked down to the bathrooms, brushed our teeth, used the toilets, and collectively decided to sleep in our day clothes, just in case.

Inside the tent, Janae, my second oldest, stayed quietly alert. Her sensitive nervous system tuned to every sound and shift in the night. Ashton, the oldest, carried his calm the way he always had, grounded and steady, watching without tension. Logan and Abigail, the two youngest, didn't question any of it at all, surrendering to sleep with the easy trust that comes from knowing they were held in their mommy's care.

I positioned myself in front of the tent door, as though woodland creatures respected such boundaries 😂, bear mace nearby and car keys clenched in my hand, convinced those jagged edges were useful somehow.

First came the bullfrogs, their chorus filling the night, then a strange crying echoing across the lake that I would later learn belonged to foxes. Just as I began to drift, Janae whispered that she thought she heard a bear. Ashton peered out the mesh window, and together we listened until he spotted the true culprit, a small armadillo rummaging peacefully through the brush. That felt reassuring. If an armadillo felt safe, we could too.

We all fell asleep quickly after that, only to wake what felt like minutes later to aggressive pawing at the zipper. Remembering my van sat right beside us, I hit the alarm on the key fob, sending whatever was outside scrambling away in panicked screeching protest. Our raccoon friend had returned and clearly regretted his decision.

After that, either the car alarm cleared the forest entirely, or I was too exhausted to notice, because I slept through a windstorm and light rain that pressed the tent walls in around us like a damp hug.

Morning arrived quietly. We woke to the brief sound of another car pulling in, tossing trash, and leaving again. When we crawled out of the tent, the lake stood before us fully illuminated, breathtaking and calm, a beauty we had no idea we'd been sleeping beside.

We gathered ourselves, walked back to the bathrooms, and then I made breakfast, successfully excluding all raccoons this time, while the kids explored the shoreline with the joy that only comes from surviving something together.

What became one of the worst nights of sleep we'd ever had turned into one of our most memorable camping experiences, and we lived to tell the story, which felt like a win all around. 😉

A BEARY SCAREY NIGHT
By Christie Marie

A warm, sultry wind blew through the open back-seat windows of our shiny red Plymouth. My strawberry-blonde hair tangled as I sat to attention at Mom's orders.

"Sit up and look at all of this beautiful scenery." My Mom explained, "You are fortunate to be able to travel for two weeks to see views like these. Just look at those mountains."

Mom looked back again to see if we had budged. Curled up like a cat on the floor, my sister slept on.

"Diana, this is no time to take a nap. Sit up!"

Our family traveled this summer, hauling our Traveling Tepee. It was a pop-up camper with a triangular roof and canvas sides.

We entered Shenandoah National Park just before sunset. In 1962, the parks were not as crowded as they are today, and we never made reservations in advance. We stopped at the gatehouse to register for a campsite.

The ranger informed Dad, "There are no available sites left. There is a windstorm warning, so park in the general parking area for tonight. There should be a vacancy tomorrow."

It was late in the day, and a storm was heading our way. Dad was tired from a long drive and hungry. We parked under a cluster of mountain maples within walking distance of restrooms with showers.

Our needs were simple. We had a lantern and flashlights. We put bologna and mustard on bread for sandwiches, and the water was free.

Then we traipsed across the pavement to relieve ourselves and wash up. On the way back, we studied a large painted map of the park's trails and roads.

YOU ARE HERE was emphasized with a big red dot. We were not too far from several trailheads, but the dark clouds frowned on our taking a nature walk. And remember, Dad was hungry. They did not use the expression hangry in those days, but that would sum up my dad when he waited too long for a meal, especially today.

The thought of a cold sandwich had not exactly been on his radar. Without a fire pit or a picnic table, we settled for this simple fare before erecting the fiberglass top of our pop-up and snapping the canvas into place for privacy and security.

I returned the meat and condiments to our cooler inside our car. I lifted the heavy lid on the dumpster, and that is when I saw THE SIGN. What caught my eye was the picture of a bear right next to our car. Like an omen, it read, Beware of Bears!

Then, it continued to instruct us not to leave food inside trailers or tents because of the bears in this park.

"Mom," I hollered, "did you see this warning?! There are bears in this park!"

"The cooler and groceries are in the car's trunk. We'll be fine," she assured me.

We had camped in other bear country parks; I guess we will be okay. Another flash, then a loud rumble of thunder answered me.

Since hiking was out of the question and there was no campfire to build up and feed, we got ready for bed earlier than usual.

The angry gray sky grew darker, streaked with lightning, warning of the coming rain. As I watched the light show through the screen, the last flash lit up the image of a bear on the sign outside. Dad zipped the canvas and screens closed. The rain began spattering against our roof.

My parents slept soundly under their comforter atop their thin camper mattress. My little sister and I lay perpendicular to them inside our cocoon-like sleeping bags on either side of the walkway to the door.

After a few hours, I suddenly awoke to the camper moving slightly back and forth. The wind howled, the rain pelted, and my eyes opened wide as saucers. The hair on the back of my neck stood to attention…I heard a new sound… a tentative scratching that gradually grew louder as the camper moved to and fro.

I looked over at my five-year-old sister. She slept soundly. Nothing ever disturbed her except when Mom woke her every night to head to the bathroom.

I took a peek at my peaceful parents. I listened to their gentle breathing and wondered why I was the only one witnessing this attack on our flimsy dwelling. That flash of lightning that lit up the sign with the bear painted on it kept coming to mind.

How would we survive if a bear tore through the canvas and screen, our only barriers? My heart pounded as I clenched my fists. I put my pillow over my ears.

I remembered a dream I had more than once of a tiger entering our small cottage. Dad sat casually at the kitchen table like nothing was happening. Mom stood before the stove, stirring a steaming pot. They did not sense their impending doom as I did.

I hollered to warn them, and then, somehow, I managed to jump up and land on the top of the kitchen door that led into the laundry room. At that point, the dream ended, or I woke up. Was this dream somehow foreshadowing tonight's danger?

I could not lie still anymore. First, I tried to peek through a small opening near the screen, but all was black outside—no streetlight or moonlight.

The wind shifted, whistling as it pounded our car and trailer. There it was again, the scratching!

I am ashamed to say that I crawled underneath my parents' bed. I went back and forth, deciding whether to wake them from a dead sleep. Or should I wait until we are attacked to call out to them?

Either way, we had no way to defend ourselves. I chose not to face grumpy parents but rather to wait it out quietly, hoping it would disappear. I put my pillow over my head again, and the next thing I knew, the sun was streaming through the screen at the doorway.

I crawled back to my space by the door and noticed the empty sleeping bag on the other side. Mom and Diana had taken their ritual walk to the restroom.

Was it safe to go outside? I wondered.

Dad noticed my movement and, in his sing-song voice, told me what a beautiful day it was. I could not believe that he said nothing about our visitor last night.

Sheepishly, I asked, "Dad, did you hear anything unusual last night?"

"The rain, is that what you mean?" He questioned.

"No, Dad. Did you feel the camper shaking and hear all the scratching on our roof?" I replied.

"It was a pretty wild mountain storm, I admit," he sighed.

"Well, I am pretty sure a bear outside shook our trailer and scratched the roof last night."

"Really? Let's take a look," Dad said as he unzipped the screen.

We ventured out the door and passed the ominous signage. I pointed to the spot where I heard scratching the night before. Dad's brow wrinkled, but he grinned as he peered around the corner. We both saw the culprit at the same time.

A low overhanging branch hung near our camper. This morning, it barely touched the fiberglass, but last night, during the violent windstorm, it leaned down and scraped the top of our trailer.

I groaned, and I shook my head. I turned to gaze one more time at that posted sign.

Hmm… I think that bear on the sign grinned at me.

HEADED SOUTH
By Philip Krull

In Kodiak, Alaska, I had long awaited the moment to embark on one of the most exciting road trips of my life. My fiancée, Courtney, and her friend, Hannah, had flown from Oklahoma to accompany me on the arduous roadtrip in Bruce, my Dodge Ram pickup. Soon, I would head through Alaska and Canada on my way to my new home in Oklahoma after four years of Coast Guard duty in Alaska.

KODIAK

A mixture of emotions flowed through me. I had waited for this moment a long time, but saying goodbye to people who had become like family to me while I lived so far from my home in Texas was not easy.

Kodiak is a small town where everyone knows most of the people who live on the island, especially if you live there long enough. I lived on a Coast Guard base and attended churches in town, so when friends and families celebrated birthdays and holidays, they invited me to join them since I was single. Because of the island's isolation, people tended to form tight relationships here on Kodiak.

Before my departure from the island, a proper goodbye was necessary to remember all my varied outdoor adventures here. This called for the last campouts in the wooded mountains with close friends.

Courtney visited me in Kodiak before, but this trip would be Hannah's first time in Alaska. What better way to experience Alaska than to immerse yourself in its natural beauty?

After nearly twenty-four hours of flying and sitting in airports, the girls would later show me how determined they were to make the most of every moment.

I drove with anticipation to pick up the girls after helping a friend out. At last we were together again! I bounded toward them and hugged Courtney, excited to see them both.

This time together was momentous for Courtney and me. It officially marked the end of our long-distance relationship. What a blessing it was. This camping trip was a celebration of our new chapter in life.

Photo by Hannah Lovy

Once the girls were in the truck, there was no time to waste; everything we needed for the first night of camping had been prepared. First, we made a quick stop at my apartment to double-check everyone had the necessary gear in their backpacks for the night. Then we headed out from the base and away from town to our adventure in the mountains.

As we headed to the spot picked out for the night, my friend, Nic, who left earlier that day, had set up camp for the group's arrival.

Driving through the winding roads again revealed to me the raw beauty that Kodiak offered. Although it was early May and the emerald green had not begun to sprout on the landscape, each season seemed to have its own unique beauty.

At last, the three of us arrived at the trailhead and started working our way up the mountain toward the camp that Nic had set up. The girls powered through being sleepy from the travel. The pizza I bought the girls for the drive to the mountain didn't help with the hike up either. However, the deliciousness was worth it.

Time and time again, I told the girls we were getting closer, keeping morale high. But it didn't take long for them to catch on to what I was doing.

Nevertheless, the higher the three hiked, the more breathtaking the views became. It was hard to believe that we would soon be feasting and spending the night in such a beautiful location.

As we got closer to the spot we'd picked out in advance, I began calling out to Nic, making goofy bird noises to draw his attention. Eventually, Nic poked his head over the hill, holding a hot thermos and a bag of different teas. The group enjoyed the fruits of their labor. We celebrated the start of this trip, the last time Nic and I would see each other for a while.

An amazing sunset showed off in the mountains while we ate our delicious meal by the fire. As the sun went down, the frigid Kodiak weather began to set in. To take everyone's mind off the cold, Nic and I built up the fire to keep us all warm.

Next, I brought out some hot chocolate, and Nic took out everything needed to make one of his favorite campfire treats… "Marios". They consisted of marshmallows cooked over the fire and then dipped in peanut butter and graham cracker crumbs.

Nic and I gathered all of the food, trash, and items with any scent on them and hiked away from camp with our headlamps beaming on the path. Brown bears are not an uncommon sight on this island, and it was important to distance ourselves from anything that might attract their attention while the crew was asleep.

Once we found a suitable tree, we began tying everything to it so it hung from the branches. Everything looked good, so we worked our way back to camp through the brush, enjoying a few good laughs. I peeked out at the mountains illuminated by moonlight one last time before closing up my tent.

There was a busy agenda for the next day, so the crew woke up early and began packing up camp, then we worked our way back down towards the truck.

Everyone said goodbye to Nic once the group returned to the vehicles. It was time to head for church. There was quite a drive to get back to town, so we hurried to get ready.

After church, the group set out to collect sea glass. This was something that I found therapeutic. I enjoyed collecting these pieces to remember this special place. It meant a lot to me to share this with anyone who came to visit me on the island. It was also a good excuse to head down to this beach and socialize while collecting something this simple yet so unique that it would remind everyone of their time here on the island.

My friend Zack and his dog, Aspen, joined us mid-hunt for sea glass. Aspen began to bound around the beach, greeting everyone with excitement.

Soon it was time to meet up with yet another friend who wanted to go on one last adventure. Conner and his family planned to meet us at a trailhead for a hike.

Before setting out on the next adventure, we decided to enjoy some fellowship by having a fire on a beach near the trailhead while warming our clothes one last time.

The group planned to hike through the woods to camp under the trees that night. The woods of Kodiak are magical year-round, but when the trees are not buried under layers of snow, the moss and evergreens keep the forest alive.

Eventually, we formed quite a line hiking along the trail; the terrain and mud made it too muddy to leave. Everyone wanted to take a picture together to remember the trip by, so there was a hunt for the perfect spot for photos. Eventually, we came across a downed tree. The trunk was suspended above the ground.

Despite the risk of falling off, many of us in the group could not resist the urge to climb onto it. First, one person climbed onto it; then more and more of the group wanted to join them. This was indeed the spot that the girls had been searching for to capture the perfect picture of our group out here in the forest.

Once we finished taking pictures, everyone found creative and goofy ways to get down. Surprisingly, nobody got hurt despite the

Photo by Taylor Waite

slippery moss and shaky tree trunk.

The path went on, but there wasn't enough time in the day to complete the entire trail. It was time to begin setting up camp in a wooded spot close to town.

Rain is no stranger to the Island of Kodiak, and tonight it decided to return for a visit. It came down with increasing intensity. Thankfully, the group had anticipated and prepared for this. There was no such thing as bad weather; just having the wrong gear and the wrong attitude. The rain tonight was peaceful here in the forest. Its rhythm against the foliage began to create a soothing atmosphere while we talked and laughed around our campfire.

Photo by Courtney Owens

Before long, it was late into the night, and time to get some sleep. The sound of raindrops striking the tent helped to lull everyone to sleep.

Early, since the sun had peered over the horizon, the dog, Aspen, had been up patrolling our camping area. Then, after waking, I shook water off the rainfly that kept my tent from leaking. I draped it over some nearby bushes to dry before the rest of the group woke up.

Aspen returned from her patrol shortly afterwards and was hardly recognizable because of the mud that worked its way deep into her coat. She needed a good cleaning, but wandered around cluelessly, wanting to greet everyone. She was puzzled why nobody wanted her morning greeting to take place in their tent.

The time had finally come to say goodbye to the island of Kodiak. Again, my trusty pickup, Bruce, was loaded with our gear for the long trek south. I looked back one more time as we waited in line on the dock for our turn to drive onto the ferry for the all-night crossing to Homer, Alaska.

Saying, "See you later, Kodiak," was hard. I never like goodbyes. They are the hard parts of friendships, but the three of us made the most of the experiences I had planned for our last days on Kodiak.

Now the time had come for the arduous road trip and our new journey into this new chapter of life to begin in earnest...

Photo by Philip Krull

THE CLIFFSIDE SCARE
A secret from Lake Superior
By Jonathan Markley

The air along Lake Superior smelled like sun-warmed needles and cold, fresh spray. Jonathan, eight, carried a red Swiss Army knife tucked safely in his pocket, and his big sister, Audrey, twelve, carried the map. They were ready for an adventure.

"Stay on the marked trail!" their mom called out from the campsite, where she was busy tending to their new baby sister.

"We will!" Audrey shouted back, already leading the way toward the northern shore where the great lake stretched out like an endless ocean.

The trail hugged the edge of the water, where the soft dirt gave way to giant gray and brown rocks. These weren't just pebbles; they were the massive cliff faces of the North Shore, looking like frozen giants leaning over the white-capped waves. The higher they climbed, the more powerful the lake felt, vast and deep.

"Look at that ledge!" Jonathan pointed. About twenty feet below the main trail, a flat piece of rock jutted out over the water. It looked like a stone balcony. "I bet we could see the shipwrecks from there!"

Audrey looked at the map. It didn't say NOT to go down there. They scrambled down a narrow crevice, sliding on their bottoms until they landed with a thump on the stone balcony. The view was incredible—the horizon was so wide they could see the curve of the earth.

But when they turned to climb back up, Audrey's face went pale. The narrow crevice they had slid down was smooth and steep. Every time she tried to find a foothold, her sneakers slipped on the dusty, ancient stone.

"I can't get a grip," Audrey whispered, her voice trembling. Below them, the Great Lake's water was deep and icy. Above them, the cliff wall was too high to reach. They were stuck.

Jonathan reached into his pocket and felt the cool metal of his Swiss Army knife. He knew he couldn't use it to climb the rock, but it made him feel like a real explorer—and explorers don't panic. He looked around.

Piled in the corner of their stone balcony were several long, sturdy branches of driftwood—birch and cedar that had been tossed up by a Superior storm weeks ago. They were silver-gray and remarkably strong, but some had smaller, pokey twigs sticking out that made them hard to handle.

"I have an idea," Jonathan said. He pulled out his knife and carefully used the saw blade to trim away the sharp, snapping twigs from the largest branches. "We can't climb up, but we can go down."

"Down?" Audrey squeaked. "Into the waves?"

"No," Jonathan pointed to a lower ledge—a wide, flat shelf just five feet below them that led safely back to a pebbled beach. "If we wedge these branches into that crack in the rock, we can use them to slide down like a fire pole."

Working together, they jammed the smoothed ends of the driftwood into a deep fissure in the stone. Jonathan tested the weight. "It's solid!"

He showed Audrey how to grip the branches and shimmy down, using the wood to bridge the gap to the lower shelf. One by one, they slid down the makeshift wooden bridge. Their feet hit the colorful Superior pebbles with a satisfying crunch. The two of them ran all the way back to camp, bursting with the story of the stone balcony.

That night, as the campfire crackled, Jonathan polished his Swiss Army knife with his shirt. They had learned a big lesson: the trail is there for a reason, but the right tool and a little bit of quick thinking can solve even the rockiest of problems.

A CRUMBY NIGHT
By Christian Krull-Pluymen

One July, six of us headed out on a camping trip from Cheyenne, Wyoming, during our summer break. There was Mom, my five-year-old brother, Phil, and I, Christian, age twelve, who first traveled in my mom's red Rodeo for three days from Texas.

When we arrived in Cheyenne, my oldest brother, Nathan, had the trailer all packed with the camping gear. He was ready to leave early the very next morning. His wife, Naomy, organized the coolers and boxes with food and supplies for us and their toddler son, Alan.

On the way to Yellowstone, Nathan said that in midsummer, the elk, bison, and bears were very active. In the nine hours of driving to get to the park, all that Philip and I could talk about was how we were so excited to see bears for the first time.

Finally, we found our campsite. While the adults set up camp, I went back to the car and scrounged for any food I could leave around the campsite to attract wildlife. I spotted some Oreos in the backseat and thought those would be perfect.

Everyone was busy, even Philip, who was entertaining the baby. Since no one was paying any attention to me, I crumpled up some of the cookies and spread them outside, on the side of the tent closest to where I planned to sleep. I was the oldest of the children, but I was especially curious and mischievous.

Mom got our attention and called us over to look at a sign, "Look here. The sign is warning us not to feed bears. See over by the restrooms, do you see that lock and cage around the trash bin? There is also a warning to keep food away from our tents and to store it in the trunks of our cars. Those bins are set up with locks near the campsites because bears are like bees to honey when it comes to human trash, and they get more brazen. They come close to where we are when they smell us cooking our food."

This sparked an idea. I thought, *This is really going to be my time to see a bear! Finally! I've been waiting my whole life to see big wild animals up close.*

"Mom," I asked, "be sure to wake me up if you hear anything in the night. I will probably need to go to the restroom then."

In my mind, I imagined that tonight a bear would find those cookie crumbs outside, close to where I placed my sleeping bag next to Mom's. But I didn't tell anyone about my plan.

The next morning, Mom announced before breakfast, "In the middle of the night, I think I heard a bear right outside our tent! I heard it breathing loudly, like it was pawing at the ground. I froze in fear! I was so afraid it would try to come in!"

I gasped and said, "Really?! Why didn't you wake me up so I could see the bear!"

At which point Mom wrinkled her forehead and questioned, "Why are you so curious about seeing a bear? Why would I wake you when there could be danger? The last thing I would do is wake you and have you run outside."

"Well, I put Oreos around the outside of the tent so that I could see a real bear for sure, this time," I answered her, before thinking that this might not have been the smartest thing to say right then.

"WHAT!!"

I could see the disbelief and anger rising in my mother's and brother's faces at the same time.

"What a horrible thing to do! Didn't you realize that we could have been mauled, torn to pieces if a bear tore through our tent? We have a baby in here and our whole family!" yelled my oldest brother.

I didn't understand why they were all so upset at me. We were all okay. I only wanted to be up close, front and center with nature, like in the zoo, but without the glass, of course.

The fury rose like lava through a volcano as the adults gave me an earful for putting the whole family at risk.

I apologized, but all the way home, I came away from that camping trip wishing and daydreaming of what great fun it would've been if only I had seen that bear.

AN ARKANSAS MINI-ADVENTURE
By Courtney Owens

Phil and I had been wanting to go camping for some time after the move from Alaska. Or at least something that felt like real camping. Oklahoma is home for now, but with Phil from Alaska and me originally from Washington, our idea of camping looks a little different. Luckily, Arkansas isn't that much of a drive, and it promised trees, elevation, and just enough wilderness to feel familiar.

After work, we loaded up the truck and headed out, arriving at the trailhead when it was beginning to become dark. We threw on our backpacks and headlamps and started down the trail.

I wasn't sure where we were going, but Phil seemed pretty confident after reading the map. Eventually, we stepped off the trail to look for a place to set up our tent...only to realize we were standing in a very healthy patch of poison oak. That discovery prompted a quick relocation.

We wandered a bit farther and found a clearer spot. We set up our tent and had a few entertaining encounters with some spiders (they were so scary). We also learned something important that night: I had packed a very comfortable sleeping pad, while Phil slept on what could only be described as a very authentic earth pad. Lots of moss, fortunately! I should remember to buy him a sleeping pad for Christmas.

The next morning, we woke up with the sun and packed up camp. We hiked back to the truck to drop off our packs and then set out for the day's hike. Phil was endlessly patient while I stopped to photograph just about everything. It was warm and sunny, but we were high enough that fog still sat low in the valley, wrapping the trail in mist. It created an almost magical but spooky feeling. An awesome opportunity for some cool shots!

Along the way, we passed horseback riders who pointed us to a scenic overlook at the end of the trail. When we reached it, we decided to eat lunch in a small cave-like outlook carved into the rock. We laughed as we watched other hikers squeeze through a narrow rock passage at the cave's end to finish the trail. Eventually, it was our turn to crawl through the passage. We did so ever gracefully...cough*.

After the scramble, we emerged onto a cliffside opening with a stunning view of the river and the gorge below. Fall colors were exploding all around us, bright against the deep blue sky. Some of the horseback riders from before were crossing the river as we took in the view. It reminded me of the trail rides we went on growing up. I discovered that Phil and I shared that, and we talked about owning our own horses one day. We agreed we would need some land and a few more pennies before we started that adventure.

After soaking it all in (and carefully retracing our steps along the cliff and through the rock passage), we climbed back up the trail and returned to the truck. We celebrated our mini adventure the only appropriate way, with gushers.

It wasn't a long trip, but it was great to get away from everything for just a little bit. I enjoyed the time I spent with Phil and the chance to slow down and experience God's creation.

CAMPING ON HORSEBACK
By Jerry Linebarger

The last school bell of the year rang. So we all packed up, the eight of us. Trucks, trailers, bags, and tack. Each of us was allowed one bag, plus one saddle and bridle. At midnight, we headed out for the Gila Wilderness National Forest of New Mexico. To be more specific, we traveled to the Big G Ranch and Outfitters.

We were Texas cowboys on a fun-filled trip in the wilderness. We planned to camp for five nights in the Gila Bend area. We drove all night and arrived at the ranch by noon. YE HAW!

We were greeted by Big G himself and his daughter, another Big G. She was a well-fed young lady.

"Stretch and wash up, boys! We got to eat fast and load up," the boss ordered.

Load up meant to get two pack mules and a pack horse loaded with all the supplies the Big G Ranch had prepared for our trail ride.

"Eighteen miles to the camp!' Yelled Big G.

The first night turned out to be a cold camp, with sleeping bags on the hard, cold ground, cold sandwiches, and water.

We were six miles upriver, and the closest town was Silver City, twenty miles back over my shoulder. So, here we were, cowboyin' New Mexico style.

Sunrise came as quickly as sunset. So now, to complete the remaining twelve miles of the trip. We crossed many streams and a river at least five times. The crystal-clear water was cold and brimming with rainbow trout swimming in the river.

In my saddle bag was a small rod and reel; I was ready to catch me some trout. I took out some miniature marshmallows and baited my small hook. Soon, supper was in the saddlebag.

About five, we arrived at the campsite with just enough time to pitch tents and roast trout over an open fire. Then the stories began in earnest. We swapped tales about our riding experiences.

Larry bragged, " I can out-rope any of you!"

Of course, I laughed, "You don't stand a chance, Larry."

He was what I would call a city slicker, drugstore cowboy. The other guys all chuckled in agreement.

Sun-up was very early, and the morning breakfast was outta sight good. Coffee and more coffee were the only things on my mind.

What happened next marked the beginning of my bad trip. Nature calls early in my morning, so off to the bushes for that to happen. However, the bush turned out to be vines, and they are called poison ivy. (I am reminded of the song Poison Ivy—bad song…very bad experience for me.)

May I recommend that when you go to the bushes to take care of Nature's call, be very sure that the leaves are broad and not on a vine! Nothing happened to me on that first day, though.

That day was just a day to prove how well Larry could rope from horseback. Here is the real twist to this story. Smart Larry was riding along when he sees a brown bear, and then his city-boy stupidity showed up.

"I bet I can rope that bear!" he yelled.

We real cowboys were cracking up, "Yes, Larry, I bet you can. Go for it!" Bill joked.

Well, I"ll be! He really did rope that bear! Now, this was both scary and extremely hilarious. The bear grabbed the rope, then gave one great tug, and the horse went down along with the city boy.

Larry yelled, "Cut the rope! Cut the rope!"

So, Bill rode in and cut the rope while the bear ran off with the Big G's brand-new rope.

By the next morning, this real cowboy was not sitting in the saddle real *bueno*. For if you can fathom in your mind a very bad posterior. I do not dare go into detail. It may be satisfying to say that it was a very long ride to the ranger station!

"We've got no way to treat this rash here," said Smokey the Bear-man.

He radioed for a chopper to fly in and pick me up, take me to the Silver City Hospital.

The doctor treated me, then said, "Stay off your horse, go back to the ranch, and wait for the rest to finish their ride in three days. You should be better by then."

I knew that the two shots back there had to help, plus a gallon of calamine lotion. The doc was right. In three days, my southern hemisphere was much better.

We headed back to Texas, but this real cowboy never forgot that camping trip.

ONCE AND NEVER AGAIN
By Betty Kocher Lusk

I just got off the phone with your Dad," I told my two girls, "and he's all finished with his classes, so we are going to go get him and then go camping! So, pack your clothes for the trip! We will be gone about eight days."

The girls squealed at the news. It had been a long, quiet summer for them without their dad around. He was working on his doctorate in music-performing arts at Indiana University. It has a great reputation for its music program. But here we were in Houghton, New York, far from the loving husband and father. I miss him so. But not for long.

This plan of mine was going to challenge me. I was used to my husband, Frank, loading the supplies and driving with a trailer hitched to the back. I made the lists and menus, shopped, prepared the cooler of food, filled boxes with cereal, oatmeal, peanut butter, bread, raisins, nuts, you know, the food that didn't need refrigeration.

I looked through the bookshelf for the big Rand McNally map book and found the pages where I had already charted our course for possible places to camp along the way. Yes, there it all was! And now to remember the route from our town in Western New York to Bloomington, Indiana.

My clothes had already been packed. I was anticipating this day, and finally it was here! Opening my closet, I pulled out my suitcase and looked over my wardrobe to decide what I would wear today for my long-awaited rendezvous with the love of my life.

I picked out a favorite outfit that Frank admired when I wore it. That done, I went out and opened up the camper, a Traveling Teepee. It needed a little airing out, so I filled a bucket with cleaning solution and water and crawled inside with my sponge in hand to scrub the floor before loading anything for our trip.

Then it hit me, I don't know how to hook up this trailer! Oh dear! It is probably really heavy too. I glanced over at my neighbor's house and noticed that Mr. Fiedler's truck was in the drive, so I walked over and rang the doorbell. They were good neighbors who took care of my youngest, Diana, who was in

Kindergarten last year from the time she got off the bus until we came home from work at the college.

Mr. Fiedler opened the door with a big grin and asked me in. The smell of sugar cookies was always in the air in this home. I quickly told him my dilemma, and he offered to hitch the trailer to my car right away. I asked if he could come a little later so I could fill the car with gas first. He agreed.

I was too embarrassed to tell him that I didn't know how to back up the trailer when it was behind the car, so stopping at gas stations was challenging enough along the way. I had to find a pump where I could pull all the way in and keep going straight out of the station after the attendant filled my tank and washed my windows.

The next morning, I woke Christine, age nine, and Diana, age five. They were such good girls. The only thing that took a little extra time was combing out Diana's tangles. She had a habit of rolling her head and singing before she fell asleep each night, so in the morning it took some time to get her straightened out and ready to go. Cold cereal didn't take long and was a mainstay that the kids liked, so soon we were on our way.

The miles and hours passed without any complications, to my relief. Christine sat up front and watched the traffic until her eyes got droopy for a nap on her pillow against the door. With the girls separated, the trip was much quieter, with no playing around or squabbling over territory in the back seat.

It was wonderful to see the joy on Frank's face as he came down to greet us. He carried his suitcase in one hand and a briefcase full of books and papers in the other, but set them down immediately to gather me in his arms. Oh, how I have missed this sweet man! It's funny how you can take someone for granted until they are gone. Then all of the little things about them make you appreciate their presence again.

Well, I had planned to surprise my husband with my plan to take us all camping. When Frank asked about the camper behind the car and then started exclaiming that he couldn't wait to get home, I froze for a moment, hoping my news would be received. Luckily, he agreed that we all needed to spend time together, and as soon as he loaded his things, we were soon traveling south toward the Smoky Mountains.

We stopped at a couple of campgrounds on the way. Then, before entering the Smokies, we took a tour of the Biltmore House in Asheville. At the end of the tour, we were ready to enter the Smoky Mountain National Park for a couple of days of hiking, swimming, and sightseeing.

After leaving this beautiful area, we drove into a campground near Cumberland Falls, not far from the Smokies. Frank set up the camper, and I helped to snap the canvas to secure privacy on the front and back. After getting the stabilizers in place, the girls rolled out their sleeping bags and pulled out their pillows while Frank built a fire. I set a can of beans close beside the fire to warm while we drove for a quick look at the falls.

On our return, I thought something did not look right. When we pulled in next to the trailer, I looked out the window.

My mouth dropped, "OH NO! Look at that right side of the trailer!"

Frank frowned with the question, "What on earth happened here?"

Diana started crying.

Christine kept saying, "Mom and Dad, do we have anything else to eat? I'm really hungry."

I got out a bucket and held it out for Frank to fetch some water... a LOT of water to clean up this stuck-on mess. The can of beans had heated up and exploded all over our grill and the trailer. I wonder if the campers nearby heard all of the commotion while we were gone?

Scrubbing was taking a lot of time and effort, so I suggested Frank take the girls to the grocery store and pick up some more food. We were all really hungry by now. Frank was more than happy to buy food, and the girls were glad to get away from the mess, hoping a trip to the store with their dad meant a treat for them. Frank loved to pick up a candy bar when he was not being chaperoned by budget-minded me in the grocery store.

I stayed behind and started scrubbing some more at the stubborn, starchy mess. After a little while, my back was bothering me, so I sat in a lawn chair to rest for a bit. A nearby camper from across the road came up to me. He admitted he had been watching us since our return, saw the mess we were in, and offered his condolences. His wife was off getting fast food for them, so he invited me over.

He offered me a cup of coffee while he listened to my story of this past summer and our little surprise trip for Frank.

I accepted his hospitality, even though I had never had coffee before and never really wanted any. It was kind of him and harmless. I needed a listening ear from someone who wasn't going to tease me or judge me for putting that can of beans near the fire without even piercing the top to let out pressure when it got hot.

Well, of course, my luck, in drives Frank and the girls. Frank was fine with me chatting in the open with a neighbor camper, but when this guy offered him some coffee, too, Frank's eyebrows rose so high on his forehead. He was incredulous. My kids knew that I never drank coffee, either. But here I was drinking with a strange man.

It has been over fifty years, and I still hear the girls tell the story and laugh about the time I sat with a man while they were gone, and even drank coffee! I drank it once and never again!

HILL COUNTRY ADVENTURES
By Christie Marie

THE VISION

"Get up! We're leaving on vacation today!" Soon afterward, footsteps upstairs told me that four sets of feet were scurrying to be the first ones in the shower and dressed for our first day on the road.

It was 1985, and I wanted my children to experience something very special this vacation to take their minds off the changes of the past few months.

I was going through a metamorphosis of sorts as a newly single parent. So, carefully unfolding a state map of Texas, I highlighted my route in yellow from Rio Hondo to Garner State Park.

When I was young and still at home, my favorite summer vacations began by loading up the camper with our sleeping bags, clothes, and a cooler full of condiments and hot dogs.

My mom always chose scenic drives across the country so we could drink in the beauty of each region's diverse land and water.

Highlights of those trips for me were the talks around the campfire as it spat out sparks and crackled. Laughter drifted from one campsite to the next. Even after we were sent to bed, we were lulled to sleep by the soft sound of their conversation.

We hiked over wooded mountain trails to view waterfalls, glaciers, and lakes. Going underground into caverns gave me close-ups of another world that I had only seen in National Geographic.

So, like my parents before me, I wanted my four children, ages three to nine, to experience something different as well. No motels. No interstate highways. No TV. No phone. No AC.

Pulling into Garner State Park, the last rays of sunlight were extinguished. By the time I signed in and paid the park fees, I had to use our headlights to find the way to our campsite. As I looked ahead, lined up like an army squadron were a dozen Harleys directly across from my campsite.

I sat in the car and sized up the situation. Hmmm. After a five-hour drive with my hopeful children aboard, was I going to back out in fear for our safety, check into a motel, then head for home?

After considering my options, I decided to take a chance. Taking a deep breath after a whispered prayer, I pulled up beside our picnic table.

As soon as we exited our Lincoln Continental (we called it The Boat), all eyes were on us.

It was quiet; fires were lit up and down the way. The sound of water and the clinking of pans as they were scraped clean signaled that the supper hour was nearly over for most. With nothing else to do, my children and I were the new entertainment. It was clear I was alone with four small children. Nervously, I pushed my hair back and wondered if it had been wise to come all of this way without any other adults to back me up.

A procession of teenage boys walked our way. I greeted them guardedly, but when they expressed their boredom and offered to put up the tent for me, I exhaled. In no time flat, I watched as they expertly set it all up.

My kids helped unload our clothes and gear, then asked what we were going to eat. The camp store was closed, and there was no wood beside our fire pit to build a fire, so we scrounged around and found a few pieces of kindling, but we couldn't get it to light because it was pretty green.

So, we munched on cold hot dogs and chips. The kids seemed fine with it, but I wondered if my decision to take on this trip alone was too risky. What was I thinking?

I awoke early, soon after sunrise. It didn't take long for me to say a prayer of thanks for our safe journey and the kindness of the kids camped nearby. Just maybe things were going to work out to be a memorable time for my little trusting souls.

HILL COUNTRY ADVENTURES
By Christie Marie

EXPLORING

The wood in the picture is one thing that was missing from our campsite the night before. I'd had visions of us sitting around a blazing fire each night in my daydreams of our camping trip.

The next morning, after lining up for the restrooms with the kids, I got out the camp stove, struck a match to light the burner, then scrambled up some eggs.

The warm food was refreshing, along with the bottled orange juice. When I looked around at my young little clan, I saw their eyes sparkle amid their giggles and laughter. They had a roof over their heads and full stomachs, and in this gorgeous place. We were together on an adventure, and I detected their anticipation.

Changing clothes took a while as they took turns in the tent, and then we brushed our teeth over the spigot by our campsite before exploring the campgrounds.

We found a dance pad with a jukebox, a jail, which they played in for a while. Then, on the other side of the campgrounds, we discovered newer campsites with recently planted trees so tiny they offered no protection from the blazing afternoon sun. I was grateful I thought to ask for an older wooded area when I reserved our campsite.

We all piled into my bronze Lincoln Continental, ready to head out for Leaky, TX, the nearest town. There we planned to enjoy a relaxing lunch, to search for an ice cream parlor, and to find a man who sold firewood at a good price.

I turned the key only to hear a grinding noise and then a click. No engine started up. No power. I looked in the rearview mirror at the expectant faces and saw their smiles melt away. These were exchanged for puzzled looks and consternation.

Now what? I didn't plan on any repair bills while I was up here. This was supposed to be a low-budget vacation, full of fun in nature for the kids.

So, I pumped the gas one more time, then tried the key. Again, there was no response.

A young Hispanic father of three boys from the next campsite headed toward us. We had waved "hi" to him and his wife while we were eating. Curious, I rolled down the window.

He asked me to pop the hood on the car so he could take a look. It couldn't hurt, so I popped the hood release. After looking things over, he told us to get out of the car, said he worked on cars for a living, and thought he could fix it in about thirty minutes. (Maybe his wife rolled her eyes?)

This was unbelievable! I had just breathed a prayer asking God for help. I figured that I would have to call for a wrecker, and since we were ten miles from the nearest tow station, I had no idea how I was going to get all five of us into town, how long it might take, or what expensive parts and labor I was going to have to pay for, as well as the towing.

Twenty minutes later, he reached for some soap and went to the water tap to scrub the grease off his hands. He splashed water on his face. Then grinned at us with the pride of a champion.

Exhaling, with a big smile on my face, I thanked God silently. We all expressed our gratitude to our generous neighbor. It was so kind of him to assist us while he was relaxing with his own family.

It was nearly eleven, and the sun stood high and hot in the sky. The kids hurried to the car after my first call. We rolled out of the park, and the motor purred contentedly as if nothing had even happened. It was time to get to Leaky for that enjoyable lunch.

After eating our fill, the waitress gave us directions. We drove around for a while until we finally found the woodlot. The owner came out and warily checked us out. He asked where we were from and learned I was alone, camping with my kids.

When it came time to sell me the wood, he filled half my huge trunk and charged me only five dollars. To top it off, he also insisted that we take a huge bag of fresh peaches from one of their trees. We headed back to camp after a quick stop for groceries.

All the way back, we talked about the challenges in our short time away from home. We marveled at God's help to us three times already.

Time to cool off in the river before our supper around a sizzling fire.

HILL COUNTRY ADVENTURES
By Christie Marie

THE RIVER

Everybody's spirits were up after our trip into town. Hot food, a stop at the ice cream parlor, and plenty of wood for ten campfires in our trunk, we headed back to our campsite to change into swimsuits.

It was over ninety degrees out, and even in the shade, the sultry breeze urged us to cool off in the Frio River. I didn't have to ask the kids twice. They hurriedly changed and came out running lickety-split.

We found a shady spot near the river where it was thigh deep for the older three to get wet and ride tubes back and forth, but not too challenging for Jonathan, who was just three.

Nathan floated with Jonathan perched on his lap for a while, and then they both piled up rocks in an attempt to build a dam across one small section of the river.

The girls preferred floating. Then they lie out on their towels to sunbathe and watch the boys.

Jennie and Audrey, finally tired of lying around, took up lifting large stones and rocks under the direction of Nathan, the dam project's chief engineer.

Now, this is what I had pictured while conjuring up this little getaway a couple of months ago. A tranquil respite for all of us along the shores of the gently flowing waters, where my kids could play in the shadows of the bald cypress.

The kids were tuckered out from all of the outdoor activity at the river and piled into the Lincoln. I slowly turned to enter an overlook that was on our way back to the campgrounds. I was eager for some pictures of the kids with a view. They sleepily complied.

That accomplished, we took turns showering and dressing for what became the highlight of each day: the country dance on the dance slab. Families brought chairs, pumped coins in the vending machines for snacks and sodas, and then saved more quarters to select favorite songs from the jukebox. The adults, teens, and children danced under the starry-moonlit sky.

Strolling back to our campsite, I looked forward to this evening's campfire. We skewered some more hot dogs and roasted marshmallows. I enjoyed listening to the happy chatter around the fire.

I wish I could've had a portrait made of us sitting there. It would have been a picture of pure contentment.

HILL COUNTRY ADVENTURES
By Christie Marie

GRATITUDE

We were up late last night around the campfire, so the next morning, we all slept in until the sun heated the interior of the tent. One by one, my sleepyheads joined me around the shaded picnic table for some cereal and milk before piling into the car for a morning at the river.

After a couple of hours in the cool water, we returned to dress for our short hike in Lost Maples State Park. I put together some lunchmeat sandwiches with mayo, refilled the cooler with ice, and we got on our way.

Hiking back into the park was invigorating. We saw a baby armadillo, heard several birds, and enjoyed just being out and about in nature. Still, on the way back out, my toddler, Jonathan, had trouble keeping up and could no longer walk, so even though I was pretty tired myself, I carried him for a bit until Nathan and Jennie asked to take turns with him. He walked some more, but he'd missed his nap and was ready to fall asleep when we reached the parking lot.

This was our last full day, so we headed back early to change into something fresh. At our campsite, three guys from our home church stopped by for half an hour to make sure we were doing okay. They had driven about two hours out of their way from their job assignment in the area. It felt good to see someone familiar, and I listened as the kids chimed in to tell them about our trip so far.

Today we had to head home, so it was time to break camp. We packed up and cleaned the campsite for a departure before noon.

Finally buckled in, we headed south toward home. On our way, we stopped at a few shops in Uvalde and ate lunch at a diner. We drove for a few hours, then stopped at a roadside park to play. We meandered close to the border until after nine that night. I became really sleepy. I was not going to be able to drive the next two and a half hours home.

I saw a sign for Falcon Dam State Park. I pulled in, but I was too tired even to pitch our tent, so I pulled into a spot near a picnic table, and we spread our sleeping bags on the seats of the car, on the benches, and on the top of the picnic table.

The sound of the A/C units on the RVs beside us kept waking me up, as did the thought of someone with bad intentions coming upon us while we slept, exposed in the open. Again, I prayed. Fear left, and an uncanny peace came over me in its place, then sweet sleep.

The sunlight and chirping of the birds gently nudged me awake. The last of our food was eaten the day before, so on the road again, we watched hungrily for a place to eat.

I was way down on my cash with only a $20 bill, and my gas guzzler needed more fuel too, so I stopped at the first open place, a Dairy Queen.

Five large ice cream cones were the "healthy" breakfast I provided my tribe. Of course, they thought it was all great! Only on vacation would their mom ever let them have so much sugar this early in the day. Little did they know why.

Finally home and looking back, the scare of the motorcycles lining the road near my campsite that first night, the feeling of insecurity about my ability to pitch a tent in the dark, the breakdown of my Lincoln Continental, and, finally, the exposure of the past night at Falcon Dam really spoke to me.

As I prayed for help, I was treated with kid gloves. Rather than having to strive, help met me at every turn.

Today, I am thankful for this experience and others that have taught me about God's provision.

"Be still and know that I am God." He whispers to me when things go wild and don't make any sense.

"Be still and trust me. Just watch how I calm the storms in your life."

Don't panic. I'm with you. There's no need to fear for I'm your God. I'll give you strength. I'll help you. I'll hold you steady, keep a firm grip on you. Isaiah 41:10 (MSG)

CHASING FREEDOM
By Jennifer Markley-Maldonado

Dear Mom,

I've been thinking about that summer at Garner State Park. The one in 1985 when you packed all four of us into the old Lincoln Continental and drove north like we were chasing freedom. I didn't understand it then, but now I know what that trip meant. It was your way of giving us something beautiful when life felt heavy.

I remember the drive. The leather seats stuck to our legs, the smell of sunscreen and peanut butter sandwiches, the warm wind whipping through the windows as the flat Texas plains gave way to hills. And then, the Frio River. It shimmered like glass under the sun, and suddenly, the world felt big and full of promise.

Setting up camp was pure chaos. You are wrestling with that borrowed tent, Nathan insisting he knew what he was doing, Audrey chasing fireflies, and Jonathan toddling toward the river every chance he got. I tried to help, but mostly I laughed until my stomach hurt. Then it began to drizzle, and you looked at me with such heavy eyes.

Before I could react, male campers nearby came to our rescue, quickly setting up our tent and helping us unload everything from the car. You handed me a job.

"Jennie, keep an eye on Jonathan while I finish setting up the campsite."

I remember taking his tiny hand, feeling the weight of responsibility settle in. He looked up at me with those big eyes, trusting me completely. In that moment, I felt grown-up, as if I were part of your team, helping hold our little world together. That crooked tent stood like a victory flag, and you stood there smiling, even though I know you were exhausted.

The days were magic. The Frio was so cold it made us squeal, and we swam until our fingers wrinkled. We hiked trails that smelled of cedar and earth, found caves that felt like secrets, and at night we sat around the fire with marshmallows, sharing stories of our adventures. I can still see your face in the firelight. Tired but glowing. I remember thinking, *"She's our hero".*

And that last night at the pavilion dance—Mom, you didn't know all the steps, but you danced anyway. You spun Jonathan in your arms while Audrey tried to teach Nathan the two-step, and I stood there watching the lights twinkle above us, feeling something I couldn't name then. Maybe joy. Maybe belonging.

   When we left, the car was dusty, the cooler empty, and our skin sunburned. But we carried something priceless: a memory stitched together with laughter, river water, and your quiet courage.

   Now, all these years later, I realize that trip taught me more than I knew. Growing up wasn't easy, but that summer showed me what strength looks like—not loud or flashy, but steady and determined. It also taught me what responsibility feels like and how love makes it lighter.

        You gave us more than a vacation; you gave us proof that love can make ordinary days extraordinary. Whenever life feels heavy, I close my eyes and hear the Frio whispering, reminding me of that summer when love was enough. Thank you, Mom—for Garner, for that crooked tent, for everything.

I love you dearly.

Jennie

TO THE CENTER OF THE UNIVERSE
By Nathaniel Markley

It was a hot and steamy Colorado summer in 2011. I had just returned from my first deployment to Afghanistan. My wife and I planned a three-week camping trip to all the national parks, historic sites, and recreation areas in Colorado.

We felt a grand adventure would be the perfect way to decompress and reconnect after our long separation. There were four of us—two young boys, ages six and three, and my wife and I.

About two-and-a-half weeks into the trip, nine stops were already completed: Sand Creek Massacre and Bent's Old Fort National Historic Sites, a scenic train ride in Alamosa, Great Sand Dunes, Mesa Verde National Parks, Yucca House, Hovenweep National Monuments, Black Canyon of the Gunnison National Park, and Colorado National Monument.

The tenth stop on our trip was a drive to northwestern Colorado, home to Dinosaur National Monument, and the second-to-last stop before ending at Rocky Mountain National Park. Echo Park, located within the monument area, was to be our campsite for the next several days.

The boys stayed gainfully employed throughout the trip, completing Junior Ranger booklets and earning Junior Ranger badges unique to each park. Before we left the park, we stopped by the visitor center so the boys could turn in their completed booklets and be sworn in as Junior Rangers by the park ranger on duty.

The boys receiving their Junior Ranger badges at Rocky Mountain National Park -Photo by Naomy Markley

After the swearing-in ceremony, usually in front of all the visitors, the boys would be presented with their badges to be pinned onto their green Junior Ranger vests. Each ranger booklet is full of activities to earn a badge. By the time we arrived at Dinosaur National Monument, our youngest son had lost all interest in completing any more booklets or activities! He just wanted to run and explore and not do any more work – even if it meant not getting his badge. So, he missed out on *this* badge.

A unique feature of the Junior Ranger program is that there is no age limit, so he can return at any time to earn his badge. Maybe one day he'll return with his family to finally earn the badge he missed.

After our oldest son completed the activities and was sworn in as the newest Junior Ranger of the park, we drove twenty-five miles down Harpers Corner Road from the Canyon Visitors Center, then turned onto a red-dirt road called Echo Park Road.

Thirteen miles of steep and dusty switchbacks led us down to the Dinosaur's canyon country on the banks of the confluence of the Green and Yampa rivers. This is where the rivers flow around a massive rock formation known as Steamboat Rock, rising over a thousand vertical feet from the base of the river.

Loud voices from across the sandy banks of the opposite shore bounce off the sheer vertical face of Steamboat Rock and echo back with near-perfect clarity – hence the name, Echo Park.

The rock formation was originally named Echo Rock in an 1875 report by geographer John Wesley Powell. It wasn't until 1941 that a U.S. Geological Survey of Dinosaur National Monument labeled it "Steamboat," and it kept the name ever since. I can see how the rock looks like the massive bow of a ship steaming through the open waters, but I prefer the

Steamboat Rock -Photo by Naomy Markley

name Echo Rock, because I'll never forget all of us yelling at the tops of our lungs, waiting for the rock to return our voices. It always did.

    At this point in the trip, we haven't showered in a week. It was the middle of summer in Colorado. We were tired, hot, smelly, and excited to finally arrive at our Echo Park campsite. The sun was setting. The mosquitoes were on the hunt. We finally finished making camp and having dinner, and were ready to get cleaned up! But there were no showers at this campsite, so we decided to go down to the river and bathe.

    There was a trail leading down to a gently sloped landing where the rivers make a majestic, sharp turn in the rocky canyon. This point is just after the two rivers combine.

    There was just enough of a bank to wade knee deep and wash off with soap. A step too far into the water, and the river would take you with it. A step back closer to shore, and the water was barely moving.

    The margin of error was inches. There were no rapids, but the river was deep and swift. With two young boys, it was enough to make us hold on tight to their little hands while soaping each other off and dunking underneath to rinse. One misstep and it would be extremely difficult to recover a child, as there are no clear banks downriver to make an exit. Slipping into the swift current was not an option. This thought was paramount as we successfully bathed in the river.

After the river bath -Photo by Naomy Markley

    We felt clean. It was the first time we'd

actually bathed in a river, and despite the river flowing with light brown silt from the arid plateaus and canyons of northwestern Colorado, we were actually clean. The Echo Park canyon area campground was sure to bring a cooler night's sleep than the hot, sunbaked parks of Great Sand Dunes and Mesa Verde we had just visited. A welcome change, even if only mild.

About one mile up the red-dirt road from Echo Park is a feature in the sandstone cliffside that looks like a cave, but upon entering, it turns out to be a large fissure. The fracture in the rock ascends all the way to the top of the cliff.

Whispering Cave entrance -Photo by Naomy Markley

It's called Whispering Cave. The unique characteristic of this feature creates a draft of cool air, almost air-conditioned, which gently blows out of the "cave" entrance and is a welcome stop on a hot day. It's hard to know how long this geological feature has existed, but it will most certainly break away from the cliffside one day and be forgotten.

If, one day, you decide to visit, stand quietly at the cave entrance and listen. It's said that if you're patient enough, the sounds of dinosaurs roaming nearby or Indian warriors from long ago can be heard echoing within as if trapped between their universe and ours.

Our oldest son found a spot along the riverbank to try his hand at fishing. He was beginning to enjoy this hobby after catching his first-ever fish below the dam at the Black Canyon of the Gunnison National Park, a few stops prior. Our youngest preferred to be free and run around.

The banks at this new spot were sandy, and the strong current eroded a steep drop-off a few yards out into the waters. The spot to wade and fish was narrow, and the drop-off was unseen in the murky, silty waters. Care was taken to ensure he didn't go on an unexpected trip down the river.

We played in the beachy sand and walked for what seemed to be forever, exploring the banks. At the confluence of the Green and Yampa rivers, a visible line of green water and tan, silty water flowed parallel to each other, unmixed. It was interesting how the two rivers flowed into each other but almost refused to become one; each carrying its own identity downstream for as long as it could until finally conceding. As in any marriage, becoming one takes time.

Eventually, we came across mountain lion prints in the sand near the water and decided it was probably time to head back to camp, since the sun was quickly setting. It was getting to be that time of day when thirsty animals would come down to the river to drink, and we didn't want to remind them they were hungry, too.

Although no fish were caught this time around, and nobody was chased by wild animals, I imagine our boys will never forget the memories of us exploring, bathing, hiking, and spending time together in a special place that has weathered the echoes of time. After a few days, we packed our things and left.

These are the special moments. They are fleeting, yet eternal. It's where the majestic creation expresses the grandeur of a brilliant Creator. Where past, present, and future disappear.

Where the carnal and the divine are eternally interwoven. Where the soul is inspired, and mortality realized. Where time and space whisper quietly across the ages. Where echoes of stories long to be told.

    Where campfires are lit, and families gather around, watching a flicker of flames rebuke the enveloping darkness. Where small, dirty fingers eagerly await their roasted, chocolaty treats. Where the hustle of the day recedes into a calm, meditative stare, and stories of grand adventures unfold from the recesses of inspired minds. Where man walks with God in a garden at the center of his universe, this place, these people, the memories, are the treasures we came to find— treasures we pack with our things as we leave.

A CAMPING MISADVENTURE
By Diana Longwell

I grew up camping with my family throughout my childhood and have many great memories. This was the one time each year when my sister, Christie, and I had Mom and Dad all to ourselves. I would say these trips were among my best memories and experiences growing up. Since Mom and Dad worked in college education, they had plenty of free time in the summer, when we would take off and explore different parts of the country.

We started out with a pop-up Tee Pee trailer, basically a bed with a shelter overhead, but it was still an adventure. Later, we upgraded to a Bee Line trailer fully equipped with beds, a kitchen, and a bathroom. Most of the time, we slept inside the trailer, but on occasion, Christie and I would sleep out in our pup tent.

I loved sitting around the campfire, looking at the stars, smelling the wood burning, hearing the logs pop, and cooking hot dogs or marshmallows over the fire. I also loved hiking, and still do to this day. The thing about hiking, not only are you able to get good exercise and immerse yourself in nature, but you're able to journey to places that are off the beaten path, where you can behold hidden lakes, overlooks, or other out-of-sight gems that can only be experienced this way.

One time, I remember getting a little too close to the edge of a cliff for my parents' comfort as a curious young girl. I had fun walking barefoot in streams, leaning over to drink refreshing, cool water, and feeding the cute little Chipmunks in the woods. One night in our campground after dark, there was a bit of commotion outside. I stared apprehensively out the window of our trailer as a big brown bear lumbered through our campground. I was really glad we were behind a solid wall, not in the pup tent, that night!

Most of our experiences were good, but there were also a few unfortunate incidents. One time, we left a sealed can of baked beans too close to the campfire while we left for a bit, only to find an explosive mess upon our return. While Christie and I went with Dad to pick up something else to eat, Mom stayed behind to clean up. When we returned, we were surprised to see her sitting outside, drinking coffee with a neighboring male camper, which she NEVER did. We tease Mom about it to this day.

One morning, as we were roughing it, eating Blueberry Muffins for breakfast (because we had an oven), we heard some grumbling and griping coming from the next campsite over. We didn't know what was going on until we heard "Shut up and drink your eggs!" I guess their camp stove wasn't working. Poor kids…Another time, as Dad was working outside the trailer getting us set up, he stood up, and his head was pierced by the corner of one of our louvered windows. We spent the next few hours at the Emergency room while he got stitched up. Ouch!

Overall, since we camped, it was much more affordable to see and do many things. I loved camping, so of course I wanted to continue this tradition with my family, right? I told Don about all this, knowing he would love it just as I had and thinking of the memories that our children and we would have in the years to come. He, however, wasn't so thrilled about the idea. As the son of a citrus grower, Don began irrigating all night starting at the age of 12, so the thought of sleeping outside in nature wasn't something he had any desire to do for "fun".

One day, some friends of ours, Tom, Cheryl, and Reg, asked us to go camping with them on the Guadalupe River near Seguin, TX. They knew Don had never camped before and assured us they would make it as pleasant as possible. They were used to roughing it, but they promised they'd find a location that wasn't as rustic. Reluctantly, Don agreed to go and give it a shot.

At the time, our daughter, Hope, was about 10 months old, and we brought her along. We arrived at the campsite and started setting up the tent we were all going to share. Soon we heard "Oh no!" I guess they had planned on bringing some cots for us, but had forgotten them, so instead we'd be sleeping on the bumpy, hard ground without air mattresses. Oh well. Not the most comfortable, but we'd manage.

So, you heard how I was used to camping, but I didn't grow up roughing it. We were always in a campground, but our trailer had running water, a toilet, and a shower. We were in the great outdoors at least. Well, we discovered that the location that Tom and Cheryl were so proud to have found, which "wasn't rustic", was just one step away from that. I guess they were used to hiking and finding a campsite off the beaten path, so where we stayed was a real upgrade for them.

There was no running water; instead, we had to go down to the river to brush our teeth, wash our hair, and wash our dishes. Our bathroom was an outhouse that hadn't been serviced in a while, and when you walked in, the fumes stung your eyes as you gagged. Remember, we had a baby with us. At least I was nursing her, so I didn't have to fool with bottles and all that stuff. That night we slept-not well-but we survived the night.

The next day, we decided to go on a trip down the river. We'd brought a canoe and a kayak. The water level was really low, so it was a challenge to travel in some places. I think this was the first time that Tom had ridden in a kayak, and he kept trying to avoid flipping over, which could have been dangerous considering how shallow it was. Yes, at least we had the sense to have one of us always stay with Hope rather than take her on the river.

The second night we went to bed, hoping to get a better night's sleep than the night before. We were awakened by a rustling by the campfire.

Don started whisper-yelling, "Reg! Reg!"

He was convinced Reg was getting into the chips and making all that noise. Turns out, it was a Raccoon rummaging through our food. Rookie mistake, leaving that out. Anyway, we had a good laugh about that. I still tease Don with "Reg! Reg!" Poor Reg...

I was pretty uncomfortable throughout this trip. It wasn't an easy trip to take with a baby on board, and Don definitely had a miserable time. This was the first and last time that Don and I went camping together. I had really hoped this would be something we could experience and share as a family over the years, but it didn't work out that way. Whenever I brought up camping after this, Don would always say, "You can go camping. I'm going to stay somewhere with a comfortable bed, air conditioning, and a shower!"

What's funny... as my kids grew up and were leaving home, they both began camping and love it. I still miss the fact that we weren't able to share these types of memories and experiences as my kids grew up, but I guess it wasn't meant to be. I'm still hoping to get Don into a little more of a wilderness experience sometime in the future, but I'll be sure there's a comfortable bed, air conditioning, and a shower nearby.

BEAR TRACKS
By Christie Marie

Walking along the Fire Hole River at Midway Geyser Basin in Yellowstone Park, I scrutinized the shore to locate fresh bear tracks along the way.

Earlier, standing in a long line for the primitive toilets, I saw that the man in front of me held a can of bear spray ready for use in his hands. When I asked why he had it out, he said he was a guide and had seen bear tracks near the river earlier that day, before his hike.

With that in mind, I carefully made my way along the river to take some quick photos of the steaming geysers. With reports of bear tracks, my adrenaline surged, imagining a bear encounter.

A Native American proverb attributed to the Sioux Nation says, "We will forever be known by the tracks we leave." Those bear tracks sent a message to the guide to take precautions as he led hikers along the trail. He then shared this information with those of us who would listen and heed his warning. He left tracks of care and concern for others. I pondered this later in the day, but for now, here I was down where the bear was sighted.

My brain was immediately stimulated, conjuring stories and images from memory, and, with apprehension, I was on alert for a dangerous encounter.

Fear emanates when encountering traces of these powerful predators. Yet the opposite of this strong emotion is what humans were created to leave behind.

Love is the fragrance that dispels fear. Love tracks can be what we choose to leave behind in the minds and emotions of the people we encounter. Love speaks loudly without the accompaniment of words.

Joyful laughter, thoughtfully expressed observations, humble responses, and mannerisms changed the atmosphere.

As Philippians 2:3-4 says, rather than walking in conceit or selfish ambition, value others even more than yourself. Observe and listen. Seek to understand the others around you: value them.

Photo by Christie Marie

Verse 15 says, then you will shine among them like stars. No, not so you can stand out like somebody special, but to bring light into a dark space of someone's life. Comforting with hope and drawing them into a more peaceful place.

I sat on a bench near the river listening to the calls and songs of robins, sparrows, and cowbirds. The sky above was blue with billowy clouds sailing lazily by. How could a place so lovely be so close to danger and death?

On this day in Yellowstone, I was briefly moved when I heard about bear tracks I had never seen firsthand. Beauty soothed my soul and dissolved my anxious thoughts.

Listening to the stories of several people I traveled with over meals and during rest stops. Taking photos of one man who traveled alone so he could have memories of his visit.

Laughter and fun, as 'Jerry jokes' and the tour director's Dad jokes, spilled out throughout the day—bowed heads as we held hands with others to speak our gratitude before we ate.

Later, hugs were shared at the end with many with whom I felt a kinship after this nine-day tour. Refreshed and alive, we all waved after exchanging numbers and cards. So many places, each one represented by someone who took home a bit more joy and peace from the time spent together.

This is what life is all about. This is who we are meant to be. Leave love tracks wherever you go each day. This will change the world one by one.

ACKNOWLEDGEMENTS

First, I would like to thank my family for contributing to this wonderful collection of camping stories. Their stories added to my original seven, making this book complete.

Jerry Linebarger, husband
Betty Lusk, mother
Jennifer Markley-Maldonado, daughter
Nathaniel Markley, son
Audrey Keel, daughter
Jonathan Markley, son
Christian Krull-Pluymen, daughter
Philip Krull, son
Courtney Owens, Philip's fiancée
Diana Longwell, sister

All photos are used with permission and taken by Audrey Keel, Hannah Lovy, Taylor Waite, Courtney Owens, Philip Krull, Naomy Markley, and Christie Marie.

I would be remiss if I did not thank Ernie Lee, who is at the helm of the New Braunfels Creative Writers club. He, along with the wonderful authors who meet monthly, face-to-face or remotely, has listened to and encouraged me as a writer. From them, I have learned to have fun with a story, to tell the hard stuff, to appreciate my own unique voice, and, most of all, to share my writing with more than just them. "Get published! You can do it!!"

Thank you, family! Thank you, NBCW! Thank you, God, for pushing me to use this gift.

AUTHOR'S CORNER

This family anthology was a project that had been hatching in my mind for years, and everyone's participation brought a variety of styles and stories that enhanced the book. I am deeply grateful for all the stories I received as Christmas gifts.

This is my first published work printed into a book for public distribution. Yay!. Thank you for choosing this entertaining and informational book. It is anybody's book, but especially for all of you, potential and current happy campers.

I am married to a wonderful man, and between us we have eight children, sixteen grandchildren, and three great-grandchildren.

But I am not old. No, I feel younger than I have in years, now that I am privileged to still be involved in the work I love. Since retirement from public school teaching, I not only daydream with ideas buzzing around in my head, but I can also write and publish blogs and books for children, for inspiration, and for posterity.

Another dream of mine since I was a teenager has been to go on mission trips. I am living that dream as well; my husband and I go abroad twice a year. He preaches, and I teach women's conferences.

I also have a children's series, the Native Texans Series. That will be nearing completion in late 2026. Each book will feature settings and fictional characters from different tribes that inhabited the land South of the Red River, now called Texas. The first three titles are *Little Child's Dream, Cornflower Girl Rises,* and *The Blue-Eyed Dog.*

Keep an eye out for these as they roll out on Amazon. You can write and give me feedback on my website, but please post a review on Amazon so that others can discover this fun book of camping adventures and many others.

-Christie Marie

My initial personal blog site since 2010:
https://www.redeemed-insandouts.blogspot.com

My author's website:
www.christiemariebooks.com

Credit for the author's photo—Daniel Grove Photography

CONTRIBUTING AUTHORS
In order of appearance in this book

Audrey Keel- A writer and a mom of six who pays close attention to how people move through complexity. As one of Christie's two middle children, she learned early how to hold the center, translate emotional nuance, and keep a sense of humor when things got loud. Her work offers readers a steadier sense of inner coherence and an eye for the quiet beauty already present in ordinary life.

Philip Krull- Philip is the youngest of the author's six children and is soon to be the husband of Courtney. Presently, he is an EMT and a certified firefighter. He has been a mechanic on C-130 prop planes, a flight crew member, and has been deployed to several foreign nations. He has always sought challenge and adventure in almost every aspect of his life. He firmly believes that by taking a leap of faith, he has had some of the most rewarding experiences.

Jonathan Markley- Son of Christie, currently resides in Washington, D. C., where he serves in the United States Air Force at the Pentagon. He is a dedicated father of three beautiful girls and one handsome boy. He balances his military service with a commitment to experience all life has to offer through food, beverages, fitness, athletics, and a passion to travel alongside friends who have become family throughout his time in the Air Force. While he was a willing contributor to this project, he noted that he only provided these personal details under duress.

Christian Krull-Pluymen- A daughter of Christie's who is a free-spirited lover of the outdoors. She meets challenges head-on. She currently lives in North Carolina, where she enjoys a vibrant life with her husband, Nic, two Aussies, and six chickens. She has courage and an unwavering zest for adventure, which she uses to inspire others.

Courtney Owens- Phil's fiancée is excited to be a future member of the family. She loves traveling and taking photos, and she will never say no to chocolate. She currently resides in Oklahoma and is excited to see where God leads her and Phil.

Jerry Linebarger- First there was Jerry the Cowboy, then *Hank the Cowdog.* Years later, Jerry became Christie's husband. He has traded his rope, boots, spurs, and saddle for a Bible and has traveled from the trails of New Mexico to the Evangelist Trail, preaching Jesus, his passion. He also cracks a good joke and is number one at closing a sale.

Betty Kocher-Lusk- The mother of two girls, Christie and Diana. Betty and her husband, Frank, took the family on quite a few trips using their traveling teepee pop-up camper at first, then later traded that in for a more comfortable travel trailer. Then the girls married and left home. Betty and Frank were free to travel abroad and lived in South Africa for five years before moving to the great state of Texas, near their daughters and grandchildren. Now, Betty is ninety-five, a mother, grandmother, and great-grandmother. She is widowed and resides with Christie, Jerry, and many good memories.

Jennifer Markley-Maldonado- The oldest daughter of Christie, who currently resides in San Antonio, Texas. She serves as the Director of Client Operations at Premise Health. She has been married for 24 years and is the proud mother of two children—a daughter, a senior in college, and a son, a junior in high school. Jennifer values traveling, reading, cooking, and time with family. While camping isn't a preferred choice at this stage of her life, she admits that her childhood camping trips gave her stories worth sharing. Nowadays, she prefers the comfort of 'glamping' in a yurt when not vacationing in a hotel, condo, or rental home. Jennifer later told us she doesn't like camping or writing assignments. But didn't she write a lovely letter?

Nathaniel Markley- The oldest son of Christie, and currently resides in East Texas with his loving wife of twenty-three years. He is a proud father of two amazing young men, one of whom has given him the most precious granddaughter in the world, although each addition will be equally precious. Nathan is a retired Lieutenant Colonel in the United States Air Force. Having put his military uniform away, he now pursues his hands-on passions, working on his vehicles, building his family home, and working the land. He also enjoys writing when inspiration strikes.

Diana Longwell- Retired in South Texas, she is the devoted wife to Don, mother to Hope and Josh, and proud grandmother to Liv and Wally. Diana and her big sister, Christie, spent many memorable hours riding in the back seat of their car on family adventures. She loves spending time playing her guitar and singing, and she runs a small specialty candy business during the Christmas season.

www.ingramcontent.com/pod-product-compliance
Lightning Source LLC
Chambersburg PA
CBHW032047040426
42449CB00007B/1018